Gandhi

PEACEFUL WARRIOR

Gandhi
PEACEFUL WARRIOR

by Rae Bains
illustrated by Scott Snow

Troll Associates

Library of Congress Cataloging-in-Publication Data

Bains, Rae.
Gandhi, peaceful warrior / by Rae Bains; illustrated by Scott Snow.
p. cm.
Summary: A biography of the Indian leader whose nonviolent passive resistance tactics influenced reformers in other countries.
ISBN 0-8167-1767-2 (lib. bdg.) ISBN 0-8167-1768-0 (pbk.)
1. Gandhi, Mahatma, 1869-1948—Juvenile literature.
2. Nationalists—India—Biography—Juvenile literature.
3. Statesmen—India—Biography—Juvenile literature. [1. Gandhi, Mahatma, 1869-1948. 2. Statesmen.] I. Snow, Scott, ill.
II. Title.
DS481.G3B315 1990
054.03'5'092—dc20
[B]
[92] 89-5101

Printed in the United States of America.
10 9 8 7 6 5 4 3 2

Gandhi

PEACEFUL WARRIOR

New Delhi
INDIA
Ca
Rajkot
Porbandar
Bombay
ARABIAN SEA
BAY OF BENGAL
Madras

India is a large country in Asia. There are many millions of people living in it. Great Britain is a small country in Europe. Ten Great Britains could fit into one India, with plenty of room left over. Yet at one time tiny Great Britain ruled all of India. And just as the American colonists of 1776 wanted to be free of Great Britain, so did the people of India a century later. Independence was India's dream for many years, but without a great leader that dream would never come true.

On October 2, 1869, that leader was born. He was Mohandas Gandhi, the son of Karamchand and Putlibai Gandhi. Mohan, as the infant was called, had two older brothers and an older sister. He had lively brown eyes and big ears, and he was adored and spoiled by everyone.

The Gandhis lived in the town of Porbandar, India. Porbandar was called the white city because its houses were built of white stone. When the sun gleamed off the waters of the Arabian Sea, the town shimmered in the golden light. Porbandar was the capital of an Indian state, also called Porbandar. The state was ruled by a prince who made the laws and lived on the taxes paid by his subjects.

Mr. Gandhi was the dewan in the court of Porbandar's prince. The dewan was the prince's prime minister. He took care of the everyday affairs of government. The dewan appointed local officials, saw that the laws were obeyed, and collected taxes. He also represented the prince in all political matters with the British rulers.

The most difficult part of a dewan's job was dealing with the British. The dewan had to understand English as well as Hindi and Urdu, the main languages of India. He also had to be a wise diplomat in order to keep peace between the British and the people of his state.

If the dewan failed to do his job well, the British became angry. And when they got angry, they took the state away from the prince. This was not welcomed by the people of that state. Their prince might be a harsh ruler, but British rule was usually worse.

As the dewan of Porbandar, Mr. Gandhi was well respected and admired. Every day, people came to him for advice or for help in settling disputes. He was considered a wise and fair man. Because of this, each member of the Gandhi family was treated as a special person by the community.

Karamchand Gandhi and his family lived in a house with his five brothers and their families. It was a three-story stone building with a small courtyard and a high wall surrounding it. There were many rooms in the house, but they were quite small and dark. Karamchand, Putlibai, and their four children lived in two rooms on the ground floor. The other families lived in the rest of the house.

In the old Hindu tradition, the six families put their earnings together. All expenses were paid out of this common fund. The families always discussed how to spend their money. Even when everyone did not live under one roof, this tradition continued. All family members—parents, grand-parents, uncles, aunts, sisters, brothers, cousins—were involved in making important decisions.

When Mohandas Gandhi was a young man, he asked his family to send him to England. Gandhi wanted to study law and become an attorney. But before he could make any plans for the long and expensive journey, he had to consult his many relatives. These family discussions dragged on for months. There were questions of money, religion, and dangers posed by going to England. Finally, one uncle took charge. He convinced the family council that it was all right for Mohan to go.

Gandhi's desire to learn English law and customs began when he was still a child and his father was the dewan of Porbandar. The boy listened as his father talked about the British agents he dealt with. Many of the British thought the only intelligent people in the world were those who spoke perfect English. Well-educated Indians were still generally considered second-class if their English had an odd accent or their clothing was not bought in London. In fact, anyone who was not British was considered inferior!

Mr. Gandhi was convinced that these British prejudices were wrong. But he also knew that a successful dewan was a person who pleased the British. So he kept his feelings hidden from the outside world.

When Mohandas was an adult, he wrote, "Our household was turned upside down when my father had to attend the durbar [a state reception] during a governor's visit. . . . If I were a painter, I could paint my father's disgust and the torture on his face as he was putting his legs in his

stockings and feet into ill-fitting and uncomfortable boots." Mr. Gandhi preferred to wear Indian clothing. It was loose and light, making it comfortable in the hot Indian climate. But the British usually looked down on anyone dressed this way.

From his father, Mohandas learned about law and politics. From his mother, he learned about religion. Putlibai Gandhi was a sweet, gentle woman who smiled often and spoke kindly of others. Though she had no education, Mohan's mother knew a great deal about her religion and practiced it faithfully. For very devout Hindus like Mrs. Gandhi, religion was more than going to temple for prayers once a week. It was a way of life.

Fasting was an important part of Mrs. Gandhi's religious practice. There were two reasons for going without food: self-discipline and self-purification. Usually, fasts lasted no more than a day. But during the four-month monsoon season, when it rained day and night, the fasts lasted longer. There was a religious rule forbidding a person to eat until he or she saw the sun shining. Because of this rule, Mrs. Gandhi would often go without food for two or three days at a time. She would not give in to her hunger.

Mohan was deeply impressed by his mother's refusal to break this religious rule. Years later, he wrote, "We children on those days would stand staring at the sky, waiting to announce the appearance of the sun to our mother. I remember days when, at the sun's sudden appearance, we would rush and announce it to her. She would run out to see with her own eyes, but by that time the fugitive sun would be gone, thus depriving her of her meal. 'That does not matter,' she would say cheerfully. 'God did not want me to eat today.' "

The idea of fasting to purify the body and to show self-discipline became important in Mohandas Gandhi's adult life. He never forgot his mother's firm discipline and dedication. These qualities were like a spiritual force to people around her.

This belief stayed with Mohandas Gandhi and grew stronger with each year. He was certain that a person who denies the body's needs increases the power of the soul. This, he felt, gives a person special strength over the world around him.

But for the most part, Mohan was like any other child. He liked having fun—whether running and playing, climbing trees, or exploring the streets of Porbandar. He was supposed to stay in the

family courtyard and not wander away from the house. But Mohan was curious about the world and often ignored the rule.

One day during a religious festival, Mohan slipped into a parade that was passing his house. All day he followed a group of children who were part of the religious celebration. The hours went by and the little boy grew hungry. But he had no money to buy food. So he ate the flowers that fell from the garlands worn by the marchers.

By the time Mohan found his way home, the Gandhis were very worried. Then, when the boy said he had eaten flowers and had a terrible stomachache, his parents were terrified. What if five-year-old Mohan had eaten a poisonous plant? They sent for the family doctor, who gave the boy some medicine to work against any possible poison. Fortunately, the flowers caused nothing more than the stomachache.

After this, the Gandhis gave up trying to keep the boy in the family courtyard. Instead, they hired a nursemaid. Her instructions were to follow the boy wherever he went and to see that he did not get into trouble. Mohan enjoyed this newfound freedom.

From the age of five until he was seven years old, Mohan attended school, the local dhooli shala. *Dhooli shala* means "dust school." That is because there were no blackboards, chalk, paper, or ink. The teacher drew letters and numbers with a stick in the sand floor of the school. The children copied the teacher, each one practicing with a stick in the sand. Then they rubbed away their work and started on the next lesson.

When Mohan was seven years old, his family moved from Porbandar to Rajkot. Mr. Gandhi had been appointed dewan to the prince of Rajkot. Rajkot was a small, inland town more than a hundred miles north of Porbandar. Rajkot was not as pleasant or interesting as the city the Gandhis had left. But it was the administrative head-quarters of the entire region. That made being the

dewan of Rajkot more important than being the dewan of Porbandar.

The Gandhis' first experience with segregation came in Rajkot. The best sections of town were reserved for the British. The houses there were large, clean, and had beautiful gardens. Indians were not allowed to live in any of these houses. It did not matter how much money they had or how important they were.

The only place Indians could live was in what the British called the native town. It was a slum—crowded, dirty, and noisy. The British sections had paved roads, clean conditions, and modern conveniences. The Indians paid taxes, but no tax money was spent on the native town. So their streets were muddy and unpaved. There were no sewers, no water pipes, and no parks—none of the things the British enjoyed.

The Gandhi family lived in a crowded, run-down apartment building near the edge of the native section. It was not like their old home in Porbandar. The family was not used to living grandly, but it bothered them deeply to be treated as second-class citizens in their own country.

The cruelty and unfairness of segregation made a deep impression on young Mohan. In later years, these feelings were expressed in his fight for equality and independence for all Indians.

As a youngster, however, Mohan was most concerned with his own day-to-day life. In Rajkot, he attended a local elementary school. It was a

little better than the old dhooli shala. This school had slates and chalk for writing. The main subjects taught were arithmetic, Gujarati (the local language), and Indian geography.

After two years of primary school, Mohan was promoted to Alfred High School. It was the only secondary school in the area for Indian boys. This Indian high school was made up of both a lower school and an upper school. If they stayed in school, Indian boys progressed from the lower to the upper school at Alfred. Anyone who did well in upper school was ready for college.

Mohan was not the best student in his class, nor the worst. His greatest problem was that all subjects were taught in English. When he was grown up, Gandhi spoke out against this. Why, he asked, should Indians in India have to study in a foreign language? It made Indians feel their own languages were inferior. And that made *them* feel inferior. Gandhi believed that Indians must feel pride in their own languages, their own customs, and their own history. Only with a sense of pride could they take their rightful place as a free and independent nation.

In addition to the regular subjects that were taught in English, Mohan studied two other languages. These were Sanskrit and Persian. Sanskrit was the language of Hindu culture. Many religious and literary works were written in Sanskrit. Persian was the language of the Muslim culture in India. Any Indian who wanted to read the classical literature of the Muslim faith had to know Persian.

As he would be throughout his life, Mohan was thin and short as a high-school student. All the students had to learn gymnastics and the British game of cricket. After school, when others stayed to take part in school sports, Mohan did not. He liked to take long walks by himself or to play *gulli-danda.* That is an Indian game played by hitting a wooden peg with a stick. It is a street version of field hockey.

When Mohan was thirteen years old, he was married to Kasturbai Makanji. She was also thirteen years old. They had been engaged since they were seven years old. This was not unusual in India. Child marriages were very common. Sometimes engagements and marriages were arranged by parents right after their children were born.

Indians used marriage as a way of strengthening and uniting families. Kasturbai's father was a successful merchant in Porbandar. The Gandhi family had businesses in Porbandar. The two families had a great deal in common, and the marriage of their children pleased everyone.

The wedding itself took a week. There were visits from one family to another. There was great feasting and dancing. The days were filled with praying, singing, and the exchanging of gifts. Every relative from both families who could possibly attend came to Porbandar for the wedding. There was so much going on that Mohan and Kasturbai were almost lost in the crowd.

After the wedding ceremony, the young couple went to live with Mohan's family in Rajkot. Mohan returned to school, and Kasturbai helped her new mother-in-law take care of the house. Mohan and Kasturbai were married, but they were still children. Kasturbai was happiest with girls her own age, and Mohan preferred the company of other boys.

Mohan's best friend was Sheikh Mehtab. Mehtab was a little older than Mohan. He was a good athlete and afraid of nothing. The Gandhis, however, felt that he was a bad influence on their son. But Mohan would not listen to their warnings.

With Mehtab leading the way, the boys got into one fight after another. Mehtab was a Muslim. He was allowed to eat meat. Mohan, as a Hindu, was not. But Mehtab convinced Mohan that eating meat would make him stronger and more manly. Mohan knew it was against his faith, yet he wanted to try it. The first time he ate meat, he felt very sick and had nightmares. After that first time, however, he didn't get sick. Even so, Mohan felt very guilty. He decided that eating meat wasn't worth the shame and unhappiness it brought him. From that point on, Mohandas Gandhi became a devoted vegetarian.

In 1887, when Mohan was seventeen years old, he started college in India. At the same time, he began pleading with his family to allow him to go to school in England. The main barrier facing Mohan, however, was religious.

The Hindu religion divided Indian society into four main classes, or castes. The highest caste was priests and scholars, called Brahmans. Next came the rulers and warriors, called Kshatriyas. Below them were merchants, farmers, and craftspeople, called Vaisyas. And finally there were the servants and laborers, called Sudras. Their duty was to serve the higher castes.

Mohan's family and relatives were Vaisyas. They were worried that if Mohan went to England, he'd become an outcaste. That meant he'd lose his caste and religion—and his identity as a Hindu. Traditionally, Hindus believed they'd become outcastes if they crossed the ocean to a foreign land.

Not even the threat of becoming an outcaste, however, could stop Mohan. He vowed to remain a true Hindu wherever he was. So his family decided to let him go and to pay for his education. The family priest also agreed finally that Mohan could go. The priest said that if Mohan kept his vow, he would still be a Hindu on his return to India.

The elders of Mohan's caste did *not* agree. They said Mohan would be an outcaste from the moment he left India. As an outcaste, he would no longer exist in the eyes of his family, his friends, and his religion.

Mohandas Gandhi considered this cruel and unfair. He had never questioned the caste system before. From that day on, however, he declared war against the unfeeling harshness of the caste system—a war he fought for the rest of his life.

CIVIL DISOBEDIENCE
Thoreau
EMERSON

Mohandas Gandhi spent three years in England. In that time, he earned his law degree, improved his English, and learned Latin and French. He also learned much about the non-Indian world. He developed confidence and became comfortable in the company of the British and their customs.

While he was in England, Gandhi also began to shape the philosophy or ideas that would guide his life—and change the course of India's history. First, he studied the ideas of great Hindu, Buddhist, and Christian thinkers. He also studied the writings of two important American authors, Ralph Waldo Emerson and Henry David Thoreau.

Gandhi believed deeply that every person is of equal value. He also believed that people must fight for that equality. But they must not hurt anyone else while doing so. They must fight peacefully. Gandhi also said that an unjust law should not be obeyed. But people should not be violent in trying to change the law.

This philosophy of nonviolence is called passive resistance. It started with Gandhi's belief in what he called soul force. In the same way that his mother's fasting and spiritual strength had impressed everyone, Gandhi believed the force of goodness in any soul would have a powerful effect on others.

Mohandas Gandhi refused to obey laws he felt were unfair. Every time he committed an act of passive resistance, he was ready to go to jail. And several times he did.

Gandhi also used fasting for spiritual and political reasons. It was his way of protesting against injustice. Gandhi's belief that all Indians must have equal rights included the Untouchables. Among Hindus, the Untouchables occupied the very lowest position in society. They were looked upon as unclean and almost subhuman by all other Hindus.

Untouchables were not permitted to enter schools, temples, or even hospitals. If an Untouchable handled food, the food could not be eaten by anyone else except another Untouchable. It was even considered an act of pollution when an Untouchable's shadow touched a Hindu of higher caste.

Gandhi wanted to change all this. He renamed the Untouchables *harijans,* which means "children of God." Again and again, he begged for their equality. But the government refused to do anything. And so in August 1932, while in jail, Gandhi announced that he would soon start a fast. He vowed that the fast would not end until the Untouchables were given their rights.

The fast began in September 1932. Within a week after it started, temple doors were opened to Untouchables. They were allowed to draw water from public wells and to walk freely on public streets and roads. It was the first time the Untouchables had ever been allowed to do these things, and it was Gandhi who had made it happen.

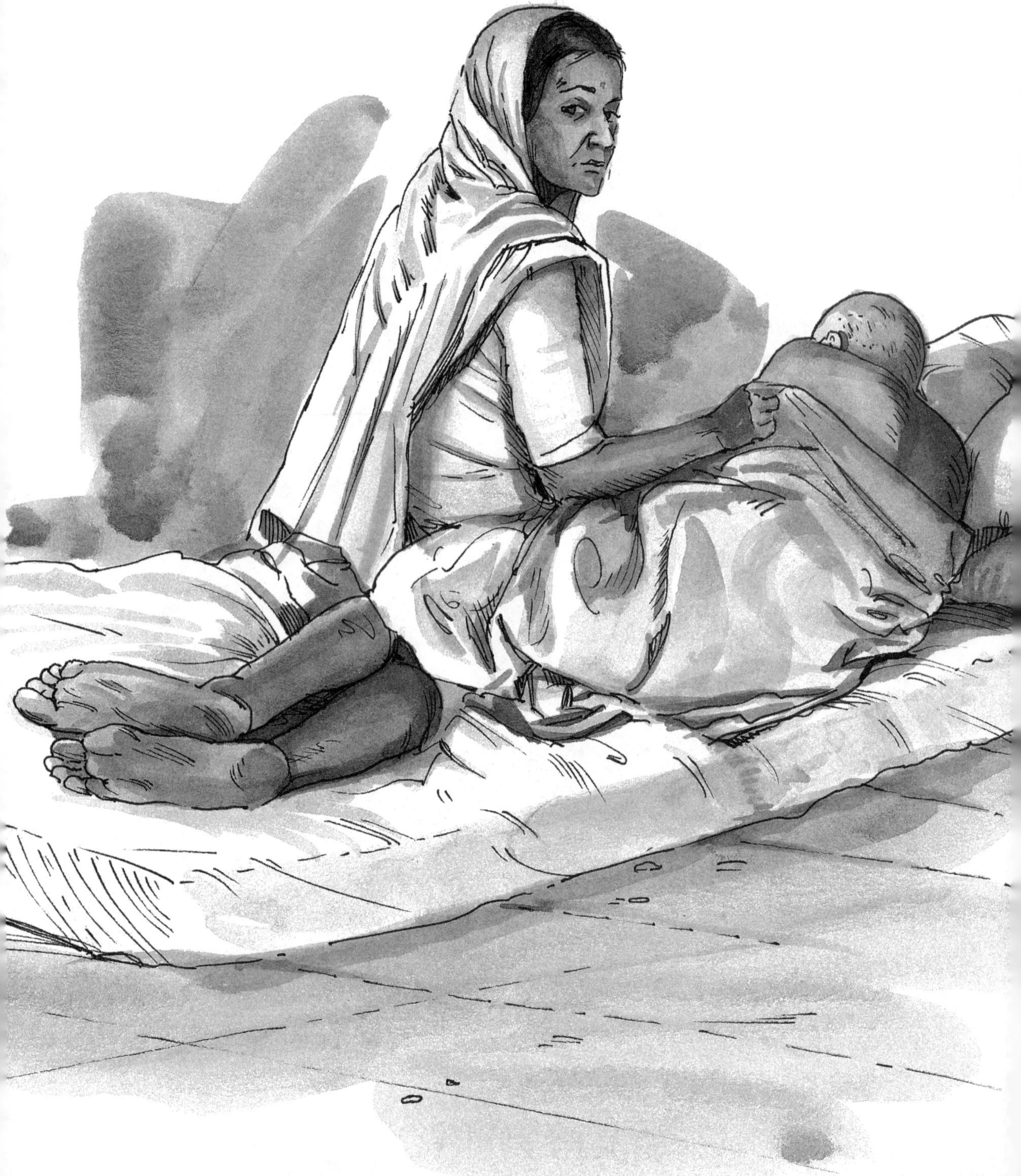

The power of Gandhi's fasts was enormous. Even though he was in prison during the 1932 fast, Gandhi's voice could not be silenced. And the next year, while he was still in prison, Gandhi was told that he must limit his writing to non-political subjects. Gandhi had an answer to this—another fast.

This fast was to last twenty-one days. Gandhi's friends and followers knew he could not possibly survive three weeks without food. The British government also knew this. And it did not want to help make a martyr of Gandhi. The British felt that a living Gandhi was a great nuisance. But a martyred Gandhi, dying for his cause, could bring about a revolution. And so the power of fasting proved victorious once more. Gandhi was released from prison. And he immediately took up the fight for Indian independence again.

Each time Mohandas Gandhi protested British rule, the caste system, unfair taxation, and other forms of tyranny, he did so peacefully. When he was arrested for his acts, he pleaded guilty. With each act of passive resistance, his fame spread and the number of his followers grew.

The first half of the twentieth century saw vast changes in India. Many of them resulted from the influence of Gandhi. He came to be known as the *Mahatma,* which means "great soul." It was said that his soul reached out and touched every Indian.

Eventually, the British released their grip on India. Independence Day for India came on August 15, 1947. Gandhi prayed and fasted all that day.

The British were defeated in India not by guns but by passive resistance, led by Gandhi. Sometimes, this passive resistance could be very simple. Gandhi wore clothes he made with the help of an Indian spinning wheel called a *charka.* It was his way of protesting the factory-made clothing of the British. And he encouraged the people of India to do the same.

Other times, the passive resistance could take on a more direct form of protest. When millions and millions of Indians refused to obey British laws and would not pay British taxes, the effect was as powerful as any cannon.

The example of Gandhi's nonviolent passive resistance made a strong impression on many others. Among them was Dr. Martin Luther King, Jr. Years later, he would lead his followers in a struggle for black equality in the United States. And Dr. King would use many of the same tactics—marches, sit-ins, and fasting—as Gandhi used before him.

On January 30, 1948, while walking to his evening prayers, Mohandas Gandhi was shot and killed by a Hindu assassin. The whole world mourned the loss of this great Indian leader and honored his memory. Perhaps Nobel Prize-winning scientist Albert Einstein summed it up best, calling Gandhi "a beacon for generations to come."